D1246341

in her words

angela bressett

a poetry book for women commemorating the
triumphs of the female spirit

Contents

OTHER AVAILABLE TITLES

A Mother's Whisper

Cupid in the Cloud

Angela Bressett

Cover design by nskvsky
Book design by Angela Bressett

Angela Bressett

Printed in the United States of America

First Printing: May 2023
Revised Printing:
New Prosperity Publishing

ASIN-

Preface

Dear Poetry Lover,

In a world where the voices of women are often silenced or overlooked, "In Her Words" is a celebration of the power, resilience, and beauty of the feminine spirit. Through the unique and deeply personal lens of Angela Bressett, this collection of unstructured free verses delves into the complexities of womanhood, exploring the joys, sorrows, triumphs, and challenges that define our lives.

Drawing from real-life experiences, Angela Bressett weaves together a tapestry of emotions and insights, inviting readers on a journey of self-discovery and reflection. Each verse in this collection stands as a testament to the strength and wisdom that comes from overcoming adversity, embracing vulnerability, and nurturing our connections with one another.

As you immerse yourself in these verses, you may find echoes of your own story, resonating with the shared struggles, dreams, and aspirations that connect us all. "In Her Words" is not just a collection of poetry, but an invitation to discover the beauty and strength within each of us and to honor the sisterhood that unites us.

It is my hope that, as you delve into the pages of "In Her Words," you will find solace, inspiration, and a renewed sense of empowerment. May the words of Angela Bressett serve as a beacon of light, illuminating the beauty of our shared experiences and the indomitable spirit of women everywhere.

Angela Bressett

Welcome to this journey, dear reader. May you find comfort, strength, and inspiration in the words that lie within.

Best wishes,

Angela Bressett

Maidenhood

Angela Bressett

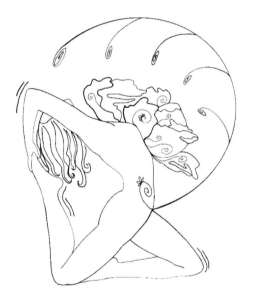

In Her Words

In the mirror, I gaze,
a stranger peers back,
no longer a child,
the flower of youth blooms.
This metamorphosis,
a cocoon of uncertainty,
I navigate the labyrinth,
of tender skin and insecurities.
Yet, in the face of change,
I find solace in the moon,
a constant presence,
guiding me through the shadows.
With each lunar phase,
I embrace transformation,
a symphony of growth,
whispering secrets of womanhood.

Angela Bressett

Lines etch my skin,
as I stretch toward the sky,
growing pains,
a testament to my becoming.
A tapestry of emotions,
woven from threads of uncertainty,
the fabric of my soul,
evolves with every heartbeat.
The chrysalis cracks,
and I emerge,
my newfound wings,
a celebration of my journey.
In flight, I discover,
the world within and beyond,
a mosaic of self,
unraveling the essence of womanhood.

In Her Words

I whisper the language of emotion,
a silent symphony,
resonating through the chambers,
of my ever-evolving heart.
For each beat is a dance,
a pas de deux,
between innocence and desire,
a delicate balance,
where love and loss entwine.
Through the crescendo,
I find solace in the silence,
a quiet moment,
to rediscover the strength,
that lies within the fragile heart,
embracing the resilience of womanhood.

Angela Bressett

Hormones flood my veins,
a tempest of emotion,
raging within,
the caverns of my soul.
A tidal wave of vulnerability,
I navigate uncharted waters,
seeking refuge in the harmony,
of my newfound identity.
In the eye of the storm,
I uncover the calm,
the beacon of wisdom,
illuminating my path.
Embracing the tempest,
I find my true self,
the essence of womanhood,
an unstoppable force of nature.

In Her Words

The first crimson tide,
a rite of passage,
uniting women across the sands of time.
In this shared experience,
I find solace,
sisters in blood and spirit,
a legacy of resilience and strength.
Through the pain,
I uncover wisdom,
the whispers of generations,
echoing in the walls of my soul.
Embracing the sacred cycle,
I am reborn,
a dance of life and death,
the eternal rhythm of womanhood.

Eyes of the world,
rest upon me,
expectations weigh heavy,
on shoulders still growing.
The chasm between,
girl and woman,
a bridge I must cross,
with trembling steps.
But in the unknown,
I find courage,
a fire kindled within,
burning away doubt.
I forge my own path,
the compass of my heart,
guiding me to embrace,
the fearless woman I become.

In Her Words

A mirror of emotion,
my face betrays me,
blushing hues,
a canvas of vulnerability.
With each shade,
a new facet of self,
a prism of feelings,
unraveling the mystery,
of my evolving identity.
In these colors,
I find solace,
the language of womanhood,
painted across my cheeks,
a kaleidoscope of truth,
beyond the veil of youth.

Angela Bressett

The whispers of change,
echo through the halls,
of my once familiar sanctuary,
my body, a temple,
transformed.
With every breath,
the walls shift,
an evolving landscape,
mapping the contours,
of womanhood.
In this sacred space,
I discover wisdom,
a testament to growth,
the architecture of self,
built upon the foundation,
of my resilient spirit.

In Her Words

A symphony of voices,
fills my ears,
advice and expectation,
a cacophony of sound.
Yet in the noise,
I find my own melody,
a song of self-discovery,
etched in my soul.
I harmonize with the world,
but dance to my own rhythm,
a waltz of womanhood,
orchestrated by the beat,
of my unapologetic heart,
embracing the music of my truth.

Angela Bressett

I stand at the shore,
a realm of innocence behind,
the vast ocean ahead,
swells with uncertainty.
I plunge into the waves,
embracing the unknown,
and as I emerge,
the salt stings my wounds,
but the water cleanses,
a baptism of womanhood,
each droplet a revelation,
that I am the captain,
of my own destiny.

In Her Words

The cocoon of childhood,
slowly unravels,
exposing me to the winds,
of change.
My wings, fragile,
yet yearning for flight,
as I hover at the precipice,
of newfound freedom.
In my metamorphosis,
I find strength,
a realization that,
with every beat of my wings,
I create the wind,
to carry me forward,
into the skies of womanhood.

Beneath the shadow,
of a crescent moon,
I whisper my secrets,
to the night.
The darkness listens,
holding my fears,
and the dreams,
that nestle within,
my ever-changing heart.
In the silence,
I find solace,
the wisdom that comes,
from listening to my soul,
as it sings the song,
of a woman,
coming into her own.

Love and Heartbreak

Angela Bressett

In Her Words

I dipped my fingers,
in the well of love,
hesitant and trembling,
like the first touch,
of morning dew.
Each droplet clung,
to my skin,
a silent vow,
to cherish the heart,
I held in my hands.
In the reflection,
of these shimmering pools,
I discovered,
that love is not,
the possession,
of another's soul,
but the freedom,
to grow together,
as the sun climbs the sky.

Angela Bressett

I am a flame,
burning with desire,
craving the warmth,
of another's touch.
But as our hands meet,
and our fingers intertwine,
I find my fire,
illuminating the shadows,
of a once hidden truth.
Love, in all its passion,
does not consume,
but ignites,
the light within us,
casting away the darkness,
and guiding our hearts,
to a place of unity,
where two souls,
shine as one.

In Her Words

I stood in the storm,
of heartbreak,
raindrops laced,
with the bitter taste,
of loss.
Each tear that fell,
carved a river,
through the landscape,
of my soul.
But as the clouds parted,
and the sun pierced,
the veil of sorrow,
I found solace,
in the knowledge,
that even the deepest wounds,
can be healed,
by the gentle embrace,
of time.

Angela Bressett

In the quiet of night,
our hearts whispered,
secrets of love,
like fireflies,
flickering in the darkness.
Each tender word,
a beacon,
guiding us through,
the uncharted waters,
of vulnerability.
In the intimacy,
of shared confessions,
I learned that love,
is not only the fire,
that fuels our passion,
but the steady glow,
of trust and understanding,
that illuminates,
our journey together.

In Her Words

I wove the threads,
of our love,
into a tapestry,
of memories,
each stitch,
a testament,
to the moments,
we shared.
As I traced,
the patterns,
of our entwined hearts,
I realized,
that love is not,
a flawless masterpiece,
but a mosaic,
of laughter and tears,
joys and sorrows,
the fragments,
of a life lived,
side by side.

Angela Bressett

In the garden of my heart,
grew a love,
as fierce as the wild roses,
that pierced my skin,
with their thorns.
I nurtured the blooms,
with my tears,
and with my laughter,
only to watch them wither,
and fall,
to the unforgiving earth.
But in the soil,
of my sorrow,
I discovered,
a hidden seed,
of resilience,
and as I tended,
to the fragile sprout,
I learned,
that even in loss,
love endures,
and grows anew.

Our love was a dance,
a rhythmic sway,
of bodies and souls,
each step,
a delicate balance,
of trust and surrender.
As we twirled,
through the ballroom,
of our hearts,
I found,
in the grace,
of our movements,
a profound truth.
Love is not,
the perfect harmony,
of two dancers,
but the willingness,
to stumble,
and rise again,
hand in hand,
as the music plays on.

Angela Bressett

I built walls,
around my heart,
stone upon stone,
a fortress,
to protect me,
from the searing pain,
of love lost.
But as you approached,
with tender words,
and gentle touches,
the bricks began,
to crumble,
and fall,
like autumn leaves,
on a windswept day.
In the rubble,
of my defenses,
I understood,
that love is not,
a fortress,
to hide within,
but a bridge,
that spans,
the chasms,
between our hearts.

In Her Words

I found solace,
in the silence,
between our words,
the quiet spaces,
where our love,
could breathe,
and grow.
In those hushed moments,
I uncovered,
a buried treasure,
of wisdom,
that love is not,
the thunderous roar,
of passion,
or the cacophony,
of declarations,
but the whispers,
of understanding,
that echo,
through the chambers,
of our hearts.

I traced,
the constellation,
of our love,
across the night sky,
each star,
a memory,
of the moments,
we shared.
As I gazed,
upon the celestial map,
I realized,
that love is not,
a single point,
of brilliant light,
but a vast expanse,
of infinite possibilities,
the ever-expanding universe,
of our hearts,
colliding,
and merging,
into a brilliant tapestry,
of shared existence.

Motherhood

Angela Bressett

In Her Words

I held you close,
my heart pulsing,
with a love,
I had never known,
as I whispered,
your name,
like a sacred prayer,
upon your delicate ear.
In the quiet stillness,
of your slumber,
I realized,
that motherhood,
is not the weight,
of responsibility,
but the lightness,
of loving,
beyond measure,
a soul,
that has chosen,
to walk,
this earthly path,
with mine.

Angela Bressett

In the garden,
of motherhood,
I planted seeds,
of hope,
and dreams,
for you,
my child,
and as I tended,
to the tender shoots,
I discovered,
that motherhood,
is not the art,
of shaping,
and molding,
but the courage,
to nurture,
and let grow,
the wildflower,
that blossoms,
within your soul.

In Her Words

I watched you play,
in the golden light,
of a summer's day,
your laughter,
a symphony,
of joy,
and innocence.
As I marveled,
at the beauty,
of your spirit,
I uncovered,
a hidden truth,
that motherhood,
is not the act,
of teaching,
and guiding,
but the willingness,
to learn,
from the pure wisdom,
of a child's heart.

Angela Bressett

I cradled your tears,
in the palm,
of my hand,
as you shared,
your fears,
and heartaches,
with me.
In the depths,
of your vulnerability,
I found,
a boundless strength,
and the revelation,
that motherhood,
is not the power,
to shield,
and protect,
but the grace,
to hold space,
for the storms,
that rage,
within your tender heart.

I carried you,
within me,
for nine months,
your heartbeat,
a gentle drum,
against my own.
When you emerged,
into the world,
a miracle,
of love,
and life,
I grasped,
that motherhood,
is not the creation,
of a new being,
but the weaving,
of a sacred bond,
that transcends,
time and space,
connecting,
our souls,
in an eternal dance,
of love.

Angela Bressett

In the quiet hours,
of a moonlit night,
I rocked you,
gently,
in my weary arms,
your breath,
a whisper,
of sweet serenity.
In those moments,
of bone-deep exhaustion,
I uncovered,
the essence,
of motherhood,
not the sacrifice,
of sleep,
and self,
but the gift,
of unconditional love,
that fuels,
the fire,
of a mother's heart,
in the darkest,
of nights.

I held your hand,
as you took,
your first steps,
your eyes,
a blend,
of excitement,
and uncertainty.
I guided you,
through the maze,
of life,
and in doing so,
I realized,
motherhood,
is not a tether,
to keep you close,
but a lifeline,
of love,
and support,
to help you navigate,
the boundless,
ocean,
of your own,
journey.

Angela Bressett

In the kitchen,
I stirred,
a pot,
of warmth,
and nourishment,
the aroma,
of love,
and memories,
filling the air.
With each meal,
I prepared,
for you,
my child,
I came to know,
that motherhood,
is not simply,
feeding,
and nurturing,
but a labor,
of love,
infusing,
each bite,
with the essence,
of my heart,
and soul.

I watched you grow,
from a fragile bud,
to a blossoming,
flower,
your petals,
unfurling,
with each new,
experience.
As I bore witness,
to your metamorphosis,
I grasped,
that motherhood,
is not the act,
of giving life,
but the honor,
of witnessing,
the miracle,
of transformation,
within,
the heart,
of my child.

Angela Bressett

As you spread your wings,
preparing to fly,
into the vastness,
of your destiny,
I stood,
with a heart,
both proud,
and aching.
In the space,
between,
holding on,
and letting go,
I found,
the truth,
of motherhood,
not in the final,
embrace,
or whispered,
goodbye,
but in the infinite,
love,
that transcends,
distance,
and binds,
our souls,
forevermore.

Career and Ambition

In Her Words

In the sterile halls,
of glass and steel,
I forged my path,
the echo of my heels,
a battle cry against
the silence of expectation.
Each stride, an act of defiance,
against the chains of tradition.
Through the labyrinth,
of challenges,
I carved my way,
embracing the fear,
and uncertainty.
I found in the fire of ambition,
the strength to redefine,
the limits of my own potential,
and realized the power within me,
was never in the title or prestige,
but in the courage to challenge,
the boundaries of possibility,
and write my own destiny.

Angela Bressett

As I climbed the ladder of success,
each rung, a victory over doubt,
and the voices that once whispered,
"You cannot," or "You should not."
I paused to catch my breath,
and looked below at the faces,
of those who held me back.
In that moment, I understood,
the weight of my ascent,
was not for my own glory,
but to pave a path for others,
to follow and rise above
the constraints of the past.
To show that glass ceilings
were meant to be shattered,
and together we'd build
a world of boundless opportunity.

In Her Words

I sat at the table, surrounded
by the voices of authority and opinion,
my own, a whisper amongst the cacophony
of power and tradition.
Yet, in the quiet of my resolve,
I found the courage to speak and be heard.
And I discovered that the worth of my voice
was not in its volume, but in the truth
and conviction with which I chose to speak.
For every word that challenged the norm,
I forged a path for others to follow,
igniting the flame of change
in the hearts of those who listened.

Angela Bressett

In the delicate balance of career and family,
I teetered on the edge of expectation and desire,
each choice, a sacrifice of time and love.
The scales of life, weighed down
by the burdens of responsibility.
But in the struggle to find harmony,
I unearthed the wisdom that true success
lies not in perfection, but in the grace
of accepting the imperfect beauty of a life well-lived.
For in the moments of laughter and tears,
I discovered the richness of love,
the treasure of memories,
and the true meaning of fulfillment.

In the dark of night, my thoughts tangled,
in the web of dreams deferred and roads not taken,
the ghosts of what could have been,
haunting the corners of my mind.
Yet, as the sun rose and bathed the world
in golden light, I awoke to the knowledge
that my worth was never in the sum
of my achievements or accolades.
It was in the love I gave,
the lives I touched, and the resilience
to rise again and again in the face of adversity.
For the measure of my life was not in milestones,
but in the journey, the growth,
and the unyielding spirit that carried me forward.

Angela Bressett

I walked the tightrope between ambition and guilt,
careful steps, each laden with judgment,
as I pursued my dreams in a world that told me
my place was only to nurture and support.
But as I reached the peaks of my aspirations,
I found within my heart a space for both,
to be a beacon of hope and inspiration,
while also tending the garden of love and family.
And so, I embraced the duality of my existence,
and proved that within a woman's soul,
there is room for boundless strength and endless compassion.

In the pursuit of success, I often faltered,
beneath the burden of expectations and obligation.
Yet, through each stumble and bruised ego,
I gained insight into the resilience within,
the unyielding will to rise again and soar,
to seek my destiny and redefine my worth.
In the struggle, I learned that failure is not the end,
but a stepping stone upon which greatness is built,
a lesson in humility and a testament to growth.

Angela Bressett

As the world around me clamored for more,
insatiable in its hunger for my time and energy,
I sought refuge in the quiet corners of my soul,
a sanctuary where my dreams could breathe and grow.
I discovered the importance of self-care,
to replenish and restore my spirit,
and cultivate the garden of my inner world,
that I might blossom and thrive in the external,
and find the harmony within that resonates,
between aspiration and serenity.

A chameleon in a landscape of expectations,
I molded myself to fit the roles prescribed,
a shape-shifter in the world of ambition and duty.
But the cracks in my facade revealed the truth,
the vibrant hues of my authentic self,
yearning to break free from the confines,
of the masks I wore to please others.
As I peeled away the layers of pretense,
I emerged, a phoenix reborn,
and discovered the beauty and power,
of embracing my unique identity,
and the freedom to live my truth unapologetically.

Angela Bressett

In the garden of my dreams, I planted seeds,
each one a hope, a wish, a goal to achieve,
and I tended to them with love and patience,
awaiting the day they would sprout and flourish.
But the world whispered in my ear, a siren song,
tempting me to pursue their desires,
and abandon the tender sprouts of my own aspirations.
As I fought against the pull of expectation,
I learned the power of choice, the courage,
to follow my heart and tend my own garden,
and in the end, harvest the fruits of my devotion,
to build a life rich in purpose and fulfillment.

Sisterhood

Angela Bressett

In Her Words

During life's tempest, I found shelter,
the warm embrace of sisterhood, a haven,
where I could lay my weary head and rest.
They held my hand through storms and heartache,
a lighthouse guiding me through the darkest nights.
Together, we danced beneath the moonlit sky,
celebrating the triumphs and milestones,
a tapestry of laughter and tears woven together.
In their presence, I discovered the strength,
of a bond forged in love, loyalty, and shared memories,
the ties that bind us, unbreakable and eternal.

Angela Bressett

In the garden of our friendship, we nurtured growth,
tending to each other's dreams and aspirations,
our roots intertwined, our spirits connected.
Through shared joys and sorrows, we bloomed,
a vibrant bouquet of sisterhood, unique and diverse.
And when the storms of life threatened to uproot us,
we clung to one another, steadfast and strong,
our bond a testament to resilience and love,
and in the aftermath, we flourished anew,
a symbol of hope and the power of unity.

In Her Words

As we walked the path of life, side by side,
we held each other up, a support system,
unfaltering in our commitment to one another.
Through the peaks and valleys of our journeys,
we shared the weight of our burdens and fears,
lightening the load, making the climb bearable.
In our darkest moments, we became each other's light,
illuminating the way forward, a beacon of hope,
and in the glow of our collective strength,
we found solace, and the courage to press on.

Angela Bressett

Through the ever-changing landscape of life,
we navigated the shifting sands of friendship,
as we evolved and grew, sometimes apart, sometimes
together.
But in the ebb and flow of our connection,
we learned the beauty of forgiveness and grace,
the power of empathy and understanding,
the art of letting go, and the courage to love unconditionally.
For in the rich tapestry of our sisterhood,
we found the threads of loyalty, love, and trust,
binding us together, a masterpiece of shared experience.

In the halls of my memories, I wander,
a gallery of moments, of laughter and tears,
each a precious snapshot of our sisterhood.
The milestones we shared, the secrets we whispered,
the triumphs and heartbreaks that shaped our bond.
With every step I take, I am reminded,
of the love that transcends distance and time,
the unbreakable connection that we forged,
a testament to the power of female friendship,
the enduring strength of women united by love.

Angela Bressett

I walked through the seasons of sisterhood,
embracing the warmth of summer's laughter,
our hearts ablaze with the fire of camaraderie.
We sought solace in the autumn's embrace,
a mosaic of shared memories scattered like leaves,
whispers of wisdom carried upon the wind.
In the cold of winter, we found our strength,
the ice of adversity bound us, an unyielding fortress,
and we emerged as warriors, bold and unbroken.

In Her Words

Within the circle of our sisterhood, we danced,
a choreography of love, joy, and shared triumphs.
Our laughter echoed through the twilight air,
and beneath the ever-watchful moon, we whispered,
secrets shared between the shadows and the stars.
In the sacred space of friendship, we were free,
a mosaic of women, undaunted and unafraid,
bound by the golden threads of trust and understanding.

Angela Bressett

In the tapestry of our lives, we wove together,
threads of laughter, sorrow, love, and loss.
The intricate patterns of friendship revealed,
as we journeyed through the labyrinth of womanhood.
We held each other close in the darkest moments,
and celebrated together when the sun shone again.
The warp and weft of sisterhood forever entwined,
a testament to the enduring strength of women.

As the tides of life ebbed and flowed,
our friendship, a constant anchor in the storm.
Through the murky waters of heartache and despair,
we clung to one another, our lifeline in the depths.
Together, we forged an unbreakable bond,
the power of sisterhood, a fortress against the tides,
and in the serenity of calm seas, we rejoiced,
our hearts brimming with gratitude and love.

Angela Bressett

In the chrysalis of sisterhood, we transformed,
cocooned within the warmth of understanding and
compassion.
Emerging, we spread our wings, vibrant and bold,
soaring to new heights, borne aloft by the winds of
friendship.
Together, we navigated the currents of life,
a kaleidoscope of women, a sisterhood of strength.
And in the embrace of our collective love,
we found the courage to fly and the freedom to dream.

Aging and Wisdom

Angela Bressett

In Her Words

In the mirror, my reflection speaks,
A story of years gone by,
Crow's feet etched at the edges,
My eyes, once a wild fire, now smoldering embers,
Yet they have seen the world unfold.

Silvery strands whisper secrets,
Of every storm weathered,
Every tear shed in solitude,
Of laughter so pure it shook the skies,
A woven tapestry of time.

My hands, weathered and wise,
Have held the hands of loved ones,
Carried the weight of my dreams,
Crafted a thousand stories,
And embraced the woman I've become.

Angela Bressett

Each day, time marches on,
Eager to etch lines upon my face,
A cartographer of aging,
A map of my journey, my growth,
As I learn to dance within its embrace.

The sun on my back, I recall,
Youth's folly, unburdened by wisdom,
Chasing dreams and chasing love,
But now, with measured steps,
I find beauty in the subtleties.

In the quiet moments, I have found,
A lifetime of experiences gathered,
A well of wisdom, deep and vast,
An endless source of strength,
In this dance with time's embrace.

In Her Words

As I walk the path of life,
The years, they weave their tale,
Lines upon my brow, a testimony,
Of laughter and love, of heartache and loss,
The woven tapestry of my soul.

In the stillness of the dawn,
I am the vessel of memories,
Of lifetimes lived, stories shared,
Each breath an ode to resilience,
Every heartbeat a celebration.

I wear my years with pride,
A badge of honor, a testament,
To every mountain climbed,
Every valley traversed,
A warrior in the realm of time.

Angela Bressett

My body, a canvas of time,
Each wrinkle, each scar, a brushstroke,
An artwork in progress,
A masterpiece, not yet complete,
An evolving tale of life lived.

The colors of my youth may fade,
But the hues of wisdom emerge,
A palette of experiences,
Of lessons learned, of love lost,
The vibrant shades of my soul.

My masterpiece, a testimony,
To the woman I have become,
Embracing the beauty of age,
The richness of life's tapestry,
A living, breathing work of art.

In Her Words

In the garden of my years,
Petals fall, colors fade,
Yet, within the earth, new life stirs,
A testament to time's passage,
The cycle of growth and decay.

I have been the bud, the bloom,
The wilting flower, the fallen leaf,
Yet, with each season's change,
I have learned the wisdom,
Of surrender, of rebirth.

In the twilight of my years,
I find solace in nature's wisdom,
The promise of renewal, the embrace,
Of life's enduring cycle,
A gentle reminder, I am not alone.

Angela Bressett

With every setting sun,
I gather fragments of wisdom,
The fleeting glimpses of truth,
Hidden within life's shadow play,
As the days turn into years.

My heart, a library of memories,
The pages filled with love and loss,
Of battles fought and victories won,
The lessons inked in deep,
A collection of my soul's journey.

In the quietude of twilight,
I sift through the chapters,
A curator of my own history,
Piecing together the puzzle,
Of the woman I have become.

Once, I was the raging sea,
A storm of emotions, unbridled,
Yet, time has taught me to be,
The ebbing tide, the gentle wave,
A reflection of life's vast ocean.

I have learned to bend, not break,
To yield to the winds of change,
For with every storm that passes,
I find new strength, new purpose,
The resilience of my spirit.

As I navigate the waters of age,
I embrace the calm, the serenity,
The wisdom born of experience,
A beacon of light in the darkness,
Guiding me towards the shore.

Angela Bressett

Through the looking glass of time,
I see the many faces I've worn,
The maiden, the mother, the crone,
Each a chapter in my story,
An evolution of my soul.

In the stillness of my heart,
I've embraced every incarnation,
Felt the weight of every choice,
The joy of love, the sting of loss,
The threads that bind me together.

I stand, a tapestry of time,
Each thread a memory, a lesson,
A testament to the woman I am,
Forever woven, forever changing,
A masterpiece of life's design.

In Her Words

I have danced in the rain,
Felt the sun's embrace,
Walked through the darkest night,
Only to emerge, stronger,
The phoenix of my own tale.

In the mirror of my soul,
I see the scars that mark my journey,
Each a reminder of my strength,
A testament to my resilience,
The beauty born of pain.

As I age, I understand,
That wisdom comes not from years,
But from the fires we've walked through,
The battles we've fought,
The stories we've lived.

Angela Bressett

My body, a vessel of time,
Carries within it the echoes,
Of laughter and tears, of love and loss,
A symphony of memories,
The rhythm of my life's song.

As the years pass, I've learned,
To embrace the ever-changing melody,
The harmonies of joy and sorrow,
The quiet whispers of wisdom,
A serenade of life's embrace.

In the twilight of my years,
I stand, a conductor of my fate,
Guiding the notes that form my story,
A composition of experience,
An opus of my soul's journey.

Self-Discovery and Empowerment

In Her Words

In the labyrinth of my soul,
I wandered through endless corridors,
Seeking answers to unspoken questions,
A journey into the unknown,
The mysteries of my own existence.

Each turn, a revelation,
Unveiling a piece of my truth,
The fragments of my identity,
The essence of my very being,
A puzzle waiting to be solved.

In the depths of introspection,
I found a compass within,
Guiding me through the maze,
Leading me to my authentic self,
The light amidst the darkness.

With every step I took,
I shed the weight of expectation,
Breaking free from the constraints,
Embracing the freedom of self-discovery,
A dance with my own destiny.

Angela Bressett

In the garden of my soul,
I once tended to the weeds,
The doubts that choked my growth,
The fears that stifled my bloom,
A servant to their relentless grasp.

But with the dawn of revelation,
I seized the tools of change,
Uprooting the tendrils of oppression,
Clearing the path for my blossoms,
To flourish, to thrive, to shine.

I cultivated my inner strength,
Nurturing the seeds of self-love,
Fostering the sprouts of self-worth,
Until my garden was a riot of color,
A testament to my resilience.

I became the gardener of my destiny,
Tending to the soil of my soul,
Planting the seeds of empowerment,
Reveling in the beauty of my growth,
A sanctuary of strength and love.

In Her Words

I wore the mask of conformity,
A veil to hide my true self,
To fit into the molds they crafted,
A prisoner of their expectations,
Silent and shackled by their rules.

But in the depths of my soul,
A fire was kindled, a spark,
A burning desire for liberation,
The craving for my own truth,
A rebellion against their confines.

I tore off the suffocating shroud,
Exposing the essence of my being,
Defying the rules, the constraints,
To stand naked in the light,
A masterpiece of my own design.

No longer a slave to their whims,
I found freedom in my defiance,
Embracing the authenticity within,
A declaration of my sovereignty,
A life unbound by expectation.

In the quiet of my heart,
I stumbled upon a treasure,
A hidden well of strength,
A secret buried deep,
Long forgotten, waiting to be found.

As I dug through layers of doubt,
I unearthed my true essence,
A gemstone of self-discovery,
Glowing, pulsating with life,
A spark to ignite my soul.

No longer the reflection,
Of who others wished me to be,
I stood tall, a beacon of truth,
Embracing the power within,
A force that could not be tamed.

Emerging like a seedling,
Pushing through the soil,
To greet the warmth of the sun,
Shattering the chains of expectation,
To forge a path of my own design.

In Her Words

I was once a fragile flower,
Wilting beneath the shadows,
Clinging to the comfort of the known,
Bound by the chains of fear,
A prisoner within my own walls.

But as the seasons changed,
So did the song of my soul,
A melody of transformation,
A rhythm of resilience,
The anthem of my empowerment.

I spread my wings, taking flight,
Defying the winds of doubt,
Soaring towards the heavens,
Fueled by the fire within,
A testament to my inner strength.

I found my voice, my power,
The courage to break free,
Shattering the cage that held me,
To stand tall, a force unleashed,
A warrior in my own right.

Angela Bressett

Lost in a labyrinth of choices,
I wandered through the fog,
Uncertain of my destiny,
Groping in the darkness,
For a beacon of hope, a guiding light.

With every turn, I discovered,
The fragments of who I could be,
A mosaic of possibilities,
Awaiting the touch of an artist,
To assemble a masterpiece.

In solitude, I found my voice,
A harmony of truth and freedom,
Resonating within my soul,
Filling the hollows of doubt,
With the echoes of self-assurance.

I embraced the labyrinth,
For it had shown me the way,
A journey of a thousand steps,
Each footfall leading to myself,
A newfound sense of identity.

In Her Words

Bound by the shackles of silence,
I struggled to breathe,
Suffocated by the weight,
Of unspoken words,
Trapped within my chest.

But when I shattered those chains,
I rose like a tidal wave,
A surge of strength and power,
Unleashing the fury of my heart,
In a cascade of determination.

The world tried to quiet me,
Yet, I would not be silenced,
My voice echoed through the night,
A roar of defiance,
Reverberating with unyielding resilience.

I reclaimed my truth, my essence,
And with each word spoken,
I painted the canvas of my life,
In bold strokes of empowerment,
Defiant against the tempest of suppression.

Angela Bressett

Like a chrysalis, I lingered,
Encased in a cocoon of conformity,
Molded by the hands of others,
Fashioned into a semblance,
Of their desires and expectations.

I struggled against the confines,
Feeling the pressure build,
An overwhelming urge to break free,
To cast away the layers,
That sought to define me.

At last, I emerged,
Transformed by the pain,
My wings unfurled, spanning the sky,
A brilliant display of resilience,
Rising above the limitations imposed.

I soared towards my destiny,
No longer tethered to the ground,
A being of light and freedom,
Reborn and unburdened,
From the chains of society's decree.

In Her Words

Through the mirror of self-reflection,
I gazed upon a stranger,
Her eyes, a testament of battles fought,
And the wisdom she carried,
Hidden within the depths of her soul.

A tapestry of memories,
Woven with threads of triumph and sorrow,
Intricately stitched together,
Each fiber, a part of the story,
Of who I was, who I am.

I studied the tapestry, admiring,
The complex beauty of my journey,
The lessons I'd gathered,
Along the winding road,
That led to my own self-realization.

In that mirror, I saw,
A warrior, a sage, a survivor,
And with newfound clarity,
I embraced the essence of my being,
The extraordinary tapestry of my life.

Angela Bressett

A fortress, once my refuge,
Guarding my heart, shielding my soul,
From the perceived dangers,
That lingered just beyond the walls,
I built to protect myself.

But as the sun rose, I realized,
These walls were not my sanctuary,
But a prison of my own making,
Confining me, restraining me,
From the life that lay ahead.

With courage as my hammer,
I tore down the fortress brick by brick,
Embracing the vulnerability,
That blossomed in its wake,
A testament to my true strength.

I stepped into the world,
My heart open, my spirit free,
A warrior embracing her power,
Fearless in the face of the unknown,
For I had conquered my very own fortress of fear.

Resilience and Perseverance

In Her Words

As the words cut deep,
Rejection's serrated edge,
A scar upon my heart,
The dreams I'd nurtured, crumbled,
The sting of failure, sharp.

But in the pain, I found,
A resilience untapped,
For each rejection faced,
Became a stepping stone,
On the path to greater things.

I gathered the broken pieces,
Transforming them into armor,
A shield against life's blows,
For in each disappointment,
A lesson, a strength, was born.

I emerged, emboldened,
A warrior of my own making,
For with every failure endured,
I found a courage and resilience,
That would shape my destiny.

Angela Bressett

My world shattered, splintered,
As love slipped through my fingers,
Leaving emptiness, a void,
The remnants of a heart, fractured,
A once-strong fortress, broken.

But in the depths of despair,
I discovered an inner strength,
The resilience to rebuild,
A heart stronger, wiser,
Capable of healing its own wounds.

Through the tears, the pain,
I found solace in my growth,
Embracing the lessons learned,
Forging a new path, a brighter future,
From the ashes of heartbreak's fire.

For every scar upon my heart,
Bore witness to the journey,
The resilience and courage,
To rise from the ruins,
And embrace love once more.

In Her Words

In the whirlwind of life,
I juggled the roles assigned,
Mother, partner, worker,
Each a weight upon my shoulders,
A constant, unyielding burden.

The strain threatened to consume,
To tear me apart at the seams,
But in the chaos, I found,
A resilience to endure,
To balance the many facets of life.

For in the struggle and the strife,
I learned the art of compromise,
The strength to prioritize,
And the wisdom to seek help,
When the burden became too great.

I emerged, triumphant,
A master of the delicate dance,
Finding harmony amidst the chaos,
A testament to resilience,
In the face of life's demands.

Angela Bressett

The whispers, the judgments,
A constant, unwelcome presence,
The color of my skin, my gender,
A target for bias and inequality,
An obstacle to overcome.

But instead of succumbing,
To the weight of discrimination,
I stood tall, unwavering,
Using the injustice as fuel,
To prove my worth, my strength.

In the face of adversity,
I found my voice, my power,
A resilience and determination,
To shatter the barriers imposed,
And rise above the prejudice.

For every challenge faced,
I emerged stronger, more resolute,
A warrior in my own right,
Bearing the armor of resilience,
In a world that sought to define me.

The sky grew dark, foreboding,
As grief's cold hand enveloped,
Stealing the light, the warmth,
Leaving an abyss of sorrow,
A heart, heavy with loss.

But amidst the shadows,
A flicker of resilience emerged,
A strength to carry on,
To honor the memory of love,
In every step, every breath.

Through the darkest nights,
I found solace in the stars,
A reminder that even in loss,
A light remains, eternal,
Guiding the way through the storm.

For every tear shed,
I forged a bridge of resilience,
Spanning the chasm of grief,
A testament to the power,
Of love, and the strength to endure.

Angela Bressett

In the mirror, I saw,
A reflection distorted,
By the whispers of society,
Telling me I was flawed,
Unworthy of love, acceptance.

But as I gazed upon myself,
I chose to defy their judgments,
To embrace my imperfections,
And find beauty in the unique,
The strength within my own skin.

I shed the expectations,
The shackles of comparison,
And discovered the resilience,
To love myself, unconditionally,
In a world that sought perfection.

I emerged, victorious,
A warrior for self-love,
For with each battle fought,
I found the courage and resilience,
To redefine my own beauty.

In Her Words

In the darkness, I trembled,
Fear and pain my companions,
The echoes of torment, haunting,
A soul battered and bruised,
Longing for solace, for freedom.

But in the depths of despair,
I found a spark, a will to survive,
A resilience to reclaim my life,
To break free from the chains,
That bound me to my suffering.

With each step towards the light,
I found strength in my scars,
The courage to rebuild my life,
And the resilience to heal,
The wounds inflicted upon me.

I emerged, a phoenix reborn,
A testament to survival,
For in the face of adversity,
I discovered the resilience,
To live, to thrive, once more.

Angela Bressett

Through the maze of connection,
I stumbled, faltered, and grew,
The complexities of love and friendship,
A labyrinth of lessons learned,
The triumphs and failures of life.

But in each encounter, I found,
A resilience to navigate the storm,
To cherish the bonds that endured,
And release the ties that bound,
My heart to pain and sorrow.

With every turn and twist,
I discovered the strength to adapt,
To forge new paths, new connections,
Embracing the resilience within,
To face the challenges of love.

I emerged, a beacon of growth,
Navigating the map of life,
For with each journey taken,
I found the resilience and wisdom,
To cherish the bonds that matter.

In Her Words

In the crowded room, I shrank,
A wallflower, hidden in the shadows,
Fear gripping my heart,
The weight of expectation, crushing,
A prisoner of my own anxiety.

But in the depths of my fear,
I found a resilience to rise,
To challenge the voice within,
That whispered I was unworthy,
Of love, of friendship, of belonging.

With each step towards the light,
I discovered the strength to face,
The tempest of social anxiety,
Embracing the resilience within,
To conquer the storm of doubt.

I emerged, a warrior of courage,
Defying the chains that bound me,
For with each battle fought,
I found the resilience to thrive,
In a world that once scared me.

In the grip of scarcity,
I fought to make ends meet,
The weight of responsibility,
A burden upon my weary shoulders,
The sting of financial strife.

But in the struggle, I found,
A resilience to persevere,
To weather the storms of life,
And find solace in the small joys,
That money could not buy.

With each challenge faced,
I discovered the strength to adapt,
To forge a path through hardship,
Embracing the resilience within,
To triumph over adversity.

I emerged, a survivor,
Navigating the waves of life,
For in the face of financial struggles,
I found the resilience and wisdom,
To cherish what truly matters.

Sisterhood

In Her Words

In the crossroads of my heritage,
I tread carefully, balancing,
The weight of tradition and my desires,
A tightrope walker, navigating,
Between two worlds that pull me apart.

But within the struggle, I find grace,
Learning the dance of adaptation,
The beauty of my ancestors' wisdom,
Melding with the beat of my own drum,
A symphony of identity emerges.

I claim the legacy that is mine,
A mosaic of the stories before me,
The colors of my past and my present,
A canvas painted with the hues,
Of resilience and understanding.

Angela Bressett

They tried to define me,
By the shade of my skin,
The language I spoke,
The customs I held dear,
Boundaries they drew, to confine me.

But I refused to be contained,
I tore through the veils of ignorance,
A warrior of truth and acceptance,
Fighting the battles for understanding,
For the right to exist, unapologetically.

In the face of adversity, I grew,
Stronger, wiser, and more resilient,
An unwavering spirit, unyielding,
To the pressures of conformity,
I stood my ground, embracing my truth.

In Her Words

The world whispered in my ear,
Telling me how to be, what to feel,
But I would not let them dictate,
The choices I made, the life I lived,
The person I was destined to become.

In the cacophony of voices,
I found my own, unwavering,
A lighthouse amidst the storm,
Guiding me towards the shore,
Of self-discovery and strength.

I shattered the mold they cast,
Embracing the uniqueness of my soul,
The power of my own conviction,
A force that could not be subdued,
By the limitations of their minds.

Angela Bressett

In the darkest moments,
When life brought me to my knees,
I found the strength within,
To rise, to heal, to persevere,
A testament to my resilience.

As I weathered the storm,
I discovered the beauty of my scars,
Each one, a story of survival,
A reminder of the battles fought,
And the victories that awaited me.

No longer defined by my past,
I emerged, a warrior of hope,
A beacon of light for others,
Whose journeys mirrored my own,
A sisterhood of strength and courage.

We stand, a tapestry of hues,
Each thread, unique and vibrant,
Weaving a story of sisterhood,
Bound together by our struggles,
Our triumphs, our shared humanity.

In our differences, we find strength,
A unity that transcends boundaries,
A celebration of our varied paths,
The beauty of our collective wisdom,
An anthem of love and understanding.

Together, we rise, unstoppable,
A force that defies division,
A chorus of voices, harmonious,
Singing the song of acceptance,
For a world that embraces us all.

Angela Bressett

In the heart of a bustling city,
I walk the crowded streets,
A myriad of faces and stories,
A mosaic of backgrounds and beliefs,
A journey through the world in a step.

I learn to listen, to understand,
The beauty of our differences,
The melodies of our languages,
The richness of our shared history,
And the harmony of our humanity.

As I embrace the tapestry of life,
I find my place among the threads,
A strand that connects and unites,
A bridge that spans the chasms,
Of culture, race, and identity.

In Her Words

I whispered words in foreign tongues,
Hoping to find connection,
Yet, the barrier stood tall,
A wall dividing understanding,
A challenge to overcome.

But with patience and perseverance,
I cracked the code of language,
Unlocking the door to connection,
To the shared stories of our lives,
And the wisdom of our diverse experiences.

In the newfound fluency,
I found the power of words,
To unite, to heal, to enlighten,
Bridging the gaps between us,
And celebrating our collective voice.

Angela Bressett

They tried to put me in a box,
Labeling me by their assumptions,
Stereotypes that sought to limit,
My dreams, my potential, my spirit,
A cage I refused to accept.

I shattered the confines of their minds,
Proving my worth, my strength, my resilience,
Rising above the expectations,
Of a world that doubted my abilities,
Because of the body I inhabited.

In the triumph of my defiance,
I found the power to inspire,
To challenge the status quo,
And to pave the way for others,
To break free from the chains of prejudice.

In Her Words

In the halls of power and influence,
I fought to be heard, to be seen,
A voice for the voiceless,
A champion for the underrepresented,
A warrior for equality.

The battles were fierce and unyielding,
But my spirit remained strong,
For every barrier broken,
Another door was opened,
For the generations that would follow.

In the echoes of my victories,
I found the strength to persist,
To continue the fight for justice,
For a world where every woman,
Is valued, respected, and heard.

Angela Bressett

In the garden of our lives,
We are flowers of every hue,
Each unique, each beautiful,
Blooming together in unity,
A vibrant display of diversity.

We celebrate the colors of our souls,
The languages that bind and connect,
The traditions that nourish our roots,
And the stories that weave us together,
In the tapestry of sisterhood.

In the embrace of our differences,
We find the strength to flourish,
To grow and thrive, side by side,
Cultivating a world that cherishes,
The beauty of our shared humanity.

Reflection and Gratitude

In Her Words

In the face of adversity,
I stood tall, resilient,
The fire within me burned brighter,
With each challenge, each hurdle,
I discovered my true strength.

The scars I bear are my story,
A testament to my endurance,
To the battles fought and won,
In the depths of my heart,
I am grateful for this journey.

For in the darkness, I found light,
In the struggle, I found purpose,
In the pain, I found wisdom,
And in the storms of life,
I found the power to rise.

Angela Bressett

In the woven threads of sisterhood,
I found solace and support,
The love of my sisters carried me,
Through the storms and the sorrows,
In the embrace of shared experience.

The laughter, the tears, the memories,
A bond that transcends distance and time,
A connection that nourishes the soul,
In the garden of our friendship,
I find gratitude for their love.

For in the warmth of sisterhood,
I found my tribe, my anchor,
In their presence, I found strength,
And in their unwavering faith,
I found the courage to believe.

In the soil of my struggles,
I planted the seeds of my dreams,
Watered them with sweat and tears,
And watched as they blossomed,
Into a life I now cherish.

Each challenge, a lesson learned,
Each heartache, a chance to grow,
The storms that shook my world,
Only served to strengthen my roots,
I am grateful for the journey.

For in the process of becoming,
I discovered my true potential,
In the depths of my being,
I found the power to transform,
And in the struggle, I found grace.

Angela Bressett

In the sacred role of a mother,
I found purpose and devotion,
A love that transcends all others,
The bond that connects and nurtures,
A miracle of life and love.

Through sleepless nights and selfless care,
I found strength I never knew I had,
The resilience to face any challenge,
For the sake of my child, my heart,
I am grateful for this gift.

For in the role of mother,
I found my greatest teacher,
In the eyes of my child,
I discovered the meaning of love,
And in their laughter, my joy.

In the mirror of my soul,
I saw the beauty of my being,
The imperfections that make me whole,
The strength that lies within,
A reflection of self-love and acceptance.

I learned to embrace my worth,
To cherish the light and the dark,
The journey of self-discovery,
Led me to the power of love,
I am grateful for the lessons.

For in the act of self-love,
I found the key to happiness,
In the acceptance of my flaws,
I found the beauty of my truth,
And in the love for myself,
I found the strength to soar.

In the maze of life's trials,
I navigated the twists and turns,
Overcame the obstacles before me,
With every step, I grew stronger,
Resilient, like the river's flow.

The setbacks, the heartaches, the pain,
All served as catalysts for growth,
In the face of adversity,
I found my true character,
And I am grateful for the journey.

For within the struggle,
I unearthed my inner resilience,
In the harshest of times,
I discovered my unyielding spirit,
And in the challenges, I found triumph.

In Her Words

As the years have passed,
I've woven a tapestry of experience,
The threads of life's lessons,
Interwoven with love, loss, and growth,
A beautiful mosaic of wisdom.

In the wisdom of age,
I've found solace and understanding,
A deep appreciation for life,
With each passing year, I am grateful,
For the journey and the growth.

For in the wisdom of age,
I found the keys to happiness,
In the acceptance of life's ebb and flow,
I discovered the peace within,
And in the journey, I found contentment.

Angela Bressett

In the depths of my wounds,
I found the seeds of healing,
The process of mending my heart,
A journey of self-discovery,
Of forgiveness, of letting go.

Through the pain, I found growth,
Through the tears, I found solace,
In the healing of my soul,
I am grateful for the lessons,
For the strength that I've gained.

For in the process of healing,
I found the courage to face my fears,
In the acceptance of my past,
I discovered the path to freedom,
And in the journey, I found redemption.

In Her Words

In the face of life's storms,
I have stumbled, I have fallen,
Yet, with each challenge, I've risen,
Stronger, wiser, more resilient,
A testament to my unwavering spirit.

Through the darkness, I've found light,
Through the struggle, I've found strength,
In the journey of life,
I am grateful for the ability to rise,
For the courage to face each day.

For in the act of rising,
I found the power of hope,
In the belief in my potential,
I discovered the keys to success,
And in the journey, I found victory.

Angela Bressett

In the presence of my mentors,
I found guidance and inspiration,
Their wisdom, their experience,
A beacon of light on my path,
A gift I will forever cherish.

Through their teachings, I found growth,
Through their support, I found courage,
In the journey towards my dreams,
I am grateful for their presence,
For the strength they've instilled in me.

For in the embrace of mentorship,
I discovered the power of support,
In the lessons they've shared,
I found the tools for my success,
And in the journey, I found gratitude.

In Her Words

In the journey of motherhood,
I cradled life within my womb,
A love so fierce, so powerful,
Boundless and eternal,
A testament to the strength of a woman.

Through sleepless nights and lullabies,
Through laughter, tears, and tender moments,
In this sacred role, I've flourished,
I am grateful for the blessing,
For the resilience motherhood brings.

For in the embrace of motherhood,
I discovered a love that knows no bounds,
In the guidance of tiny hands,
I found purpose and inspiration,
And in the journey, I found my truest self.

Angela Bressett

In the circle of sisterhood,
I found a bond unbreakable,
A connection that transcends time,
A tapestry of shared stories,
Of love, loss, and triumph.

Through the laughter and the tears,
Through the heartaches and the joy,
In the embrace of sisterhood,
I am grateful for the solace,
For the resilience we forge together.

For in the circle of sisterhood,
I found the power of unity,
In the support of kindred spirits,
I discovered the strength of friendship,
And in the journey, I found my sisters.

In Her Words

I wandered through life, searching,
Longing for acceptance, validation,
A reflection of my worth,
Then a revelation, a transformation,
A journey of self-love began.

In the quiet moments of solitude,
I rediscovered the essence of me,
My strengths, my beauty, my resilience,
Embracing the woman I am,
I am grateful for the love within.

For in the path of self-love,
I found my value, my voice,
In the depths of my soul,
I uncovered a strength untamed,
And in the journey, I found my heart.

Angela Bressett

In the depths of heartache,
I found myself shattered, broken,
A delicate mosaic of emotions,
Piecing together my resilience,
Emerging from the darkness whole.

Through the storm of sorrow,
I discovered a strength hidden,
In the mending of my fractured heart,
I am grateful for the healing,
For the resilience that mends the cracks.

For in the process of rebuilding,
I found the power of perseverance,
In the embrace of self-compassion,
I uncovered an unwavering spirit,
And in the journey, I found my peace.

The End

Thanks for allowing me to provide hope and inspiration in
your search for healing. I hope you enjoyed *In Her Words*
and that it exceeded your expectations. As an Indie author, I
depend on your support to spread the word about my books. I
would love to hear your thoughts.

Please leave your comments here.

Wishing you all the best,

Angela Bressett